AS AN OAK TREE GROWS

G. Brian Karas

NANCY PAULSEN BOOKS ☺ AN IMPRINT OF PENGUIN GROUP (USA)

The author wishes to thank Martin Clarke and Charles Canham for their historical and scientific facts, the Town of Clinton Historical Society for sharing their vintage postcards, and Kimba and Christian Fekete for their wonderful old oak tree.

NANCY PAULSEN BOOKS
Published by the Penguin Group
Penguin Group (USA) LLC
375 Hudson Street, New York, NY 10014

USA | Canada | UK | Ireland | Australia
New Zealand | India | South Africa | China
penguin.com
A Penguin Random House Company

Library of Congress Cataloging-in-Publication Data
Karas, G. Brian, author, illustrator. As an oak tree grows / G. Brian Karas. pages cm
Summary: "From 1775 to the present, the landscape around a lone oak tree goes through significant changes" —Provided by publisher. [1. Oak—Fiction. 2. Trees—Fiction. 3. Growth—Fiction.] I. Title.
PZ7.K1296As 2014   [E]—dc23   2013036651

Manufactured in China.
ISBN 978-0-399-25233-4
Special Markets ISBN 978-0-399-17603-6 NOT FOR RESALE
10 9 8 7 6 5 4

Design by Ryan Thomann. Text set in Maiandra Demi Bold.
The art was prepared with gouache and pencil.

This Imagination Library edition is published by Penguin Young Readers, a division of Penguin Random House, exclusively for Dolly Parton's Imagination Library, a not-for-profit program designed to inspire a love of reading and learning, sponsored in part by The Dollywood Foundation. Penguin's trade editions of this work are available wherever books are sold.

In memory of Pete Seeger

On a sunny late summer day,
a young boy planted an acorn in the ground.

Later that year, an oak tree sprouted up from the earth, into the air and light.

1775

Each fall it will shed its leaves and
each spring new ones will grow.

The boy no longer lived here. New people came and made their homes around the oak tree.
They cleared the hillsides where forests once stood.
The wood was used for building and to burn in fireplaces.

1775   1800

But the oak tree was left standing.

The oak tree had room to spread wide
and grew upward and outward.

Sometimes snow was very heavy
and a branch would break off.

As the oak tree grew, everyone and everything was on the move. Children grew. Some stayed to work on the farms and others left to work in factories. Ships came and went. Large engines rumbled along steel rails.

Birds perched in the oak tree to rest from long migrations.
Some stayed and made new homes, and others flew on.
More people arrived and built new houses and buildings.

Some years, little rain fell.
Hills and fields were dry where trees had once
stood and shaded the ground from the sun's rays.
The oak tree's roots reached far underground
for water as its leaves wilted.

Farmers conserved what little they had for thirsty livestock, until the rain fell again.

Electricity came through wires that were strung over hills and through valleys. It powered streetlamps and homes.

The land twinkled
with lights as stars
faded in the night sky.

1900

The oak tree grew slowly and steadily
while all around it life sped by.

1775 1800 1825 1850 1875

People rode in cars to go to work and visit friends, to go shopping or just for a drive.

Soon the air was filled with
jet contrails, and radio waves,

1775   1800   1825   1850   1875

and sound waves of beeping cars,
barking dogs, zooming motorboats,
whistling trains and music.

GASOLINE

The oak tree is two hundred years old. It has shed its leaves and grown new ones every year.

Animals, birds and insects have made homes
in its folds and holes and branches.

GASOLINE

The oak tree, with its strong roots, trunk and limbs, has survived many storms over its lifetime.

1775   1800   1825   1850   1875

Now a fog rolls in and a big storm is on the way.

The storm is powerful and the oak tree is
split in two. It does not survive this storm.

People come to look where the great oak tree once stood. The tree is cut into pieces to be used for furniture, firewood and mulch.

A new day dawns. Once again
the ground is warm and welcoming,
as a new oak tree grows.

Some facts about oak trees

 There are many types of oak trees. The white oak, the kind in this book, can live to be several hundred years old.

 By counting the rings on the stump of a cut tree, you can tell how old it was: one year for each ring.

 Oak trees can produce acorns when they are as young as ten years old. The hard-shelled acorn contains the seed from which a new tree grows.

 Oak trees can grow to be one hundred feet tall AND wide. Oaks are good shade trees.

 Acorns are an important food source for animals and insects, and people too.

 The wood from an oak tree is very strong and has many uses. Ships, houses, and furniture are often made from oak.